In the image

A Mother's Heart

Spirituality of a mother

Caroline Moulinet

From the same author:

How to survive 14 days in isolation, 2020.

Pause, and change your perspective, 2020.

Acknowledgements

To the mothers whom I have the privilege of accompanying on their journey and who give me the opportunity to witness the Glory of God.

To my mother who gave me life and whom I love in all her beauty and with all her weaknesses.

To the priests who, through their hands, their hearts and their souls, give us access to the treasures of the active Word of God.

To my children who are the way to the innocence of the Child Jesus, the joy of the Spirit, the impulse towards the Father.

To my husband, without whom I would not be the mother I become every day.

To all those who, from near or far, have allowed the birth of this book, I keep you in my prayers.

Preface

As a child, I didn't want to be a nurse or a fireman, I wanted to do voices in cartoons. I thought it was great to be able to bring a thousand characters to life, to give life to characters, emotions, situations, I found it fun and joyful!

Life didn't lead me to do voices in cartoons, and I didn't think it would lead me to write either! Me, a scientist, turning into an author and taking up a pen? A few people have said to me, seeing me live as a mother: "You should write! How do you always have a smile on your face? How can you be so patient? This made me, who had been so impatient of character, smile even more. As I listened to them, I could see that my patience had indeed grown. But writing...?

Then came the pandemic and the first containment. I had just created Radiance and workshops to help mothers to blossom and fulfil their vocation as mothers. Everyone had to stay at home, our meetings had to end, but I couldn't leave them like that, I wanted to help them start this new (and difficult) period on the right foot.

In the midst of homeschooling my four children, thousands of things to do, fatigue, weariness, I started to write. This was only the first step, the Lord continued to guide me with great patience and gentleness and I wrote a second book. I wanted to share more of the key points that go into shaping a united and radiant family. But again, the Lord persisted, I heard His call but I kept checking if my idea would really be better? I am making myself smile as I write this! How could my idea be better than His? However, continuing to write meant revealing a little more of the source of love living in the heart of my family. Sharing ideas is easier than sharing an experience.

Yes, sharing an experience is more difficult. Exposing oneself to the eyes of others is easier if it's about debating ideas, but when it comes to sharing one's perspective, one's experience, one's relationship with Christ... for me it was like taking a leap into the void. Surrendering myself completely, without a veil. With Radiance, I always talk about bringing light into the daily lives of mothers. In these lines, I will share with you what I keep as treasures in my heart. No barriers: only my humble experience, in Truth.

If I decide to share these few lines about my profound experience of my vocation as a mother, it is not because I am proud of myself or because I have found the magic recipe for THE perfect family. No, I haven't. It is to invite you to set out on a journey, to change your view of your vocation as a mother, to discover the treasures hidden deep in your heart. Then a relationship of boundless love comes to life and becomes a spring of peace, deep joy and light.

There are as many relationships with God as there are people in His Creation, so above all, keep what resonates with you and listen to Christ above all. His Word is the Way, the Truth and the Life for your own life, your vocation as a mother and to your family. He calls you to holiness, nothing less. He wants your perfect happiness. He has given you a family: this is your path to holiness.

I will not speak of the hearts of fathers, oh so important, the guardian hearts of the family. It would take a whole other book to talk about them! And another book to show how the hearts of the spouses, father and mother, three hearts united in one home, form a perfect image of Trinitarian love. So dear mothers, keep the fathers in your hearts as you read these lines.

Introduction

Did you say to yourself when you picked up this book: This is a very ambitious title! My mother's heart made in the image of God's heart? Really? How can my mother's heart become a vehicle for God's heart? And then, to whom can I give a taste of God's heart? To myself? To my children? Would my mother's heart be able to taste the Holy of Holies? Eternity? Infinite love? Let's take an example then.

In becoming a mother, I experienced the immensity of a mother's love. Jesus said, "*A man can have no greater love than to lay down his life for his friends.*" (John 15:13).

Intellectually, it is very beautiful. Poetic even. It is easy for it to remain at a purely intellectual understanding and to have difficulties in letting the Word descend into our heart, to let it just live in us, without dissecting it, explaining it, trying to understand it.

But when I became a mother, I had this experience: yes, if today I am asked to choose: "A person must die now. You or your child?" Me of course. Without an ounce of hesitation. It's very personal. But I don't think I'm the only one who has this impulse. A conviction rooted in my flesh. If I can suffer in my child's place, yes, I will take it upon myself to spare him or her. This is true for our lives, as well as for the little sufferings of everyday life: don't we sometimes dream of being able to prevent the sorrows of our children?

And this is where the adventure begins. That the living encounter takes place. That the very heart of God begins to reveal itself. How humble that Jesus became a little child and lowered himself to us. Christ who gave his life to save us, to allow us to be called Children of God and to give us eternal life: He is the One I must follow to understand the vocation of a mother's heart.

May these lines invite you to follow your path as a mother with simplicity and truth, filled with the confidence that God the Father is at work through your hands and your heart to shape his Kingdom. May these lines open you to the immensity that dwells within you.

I-

From conception to birth

A soul becomes flesh

How beautiful is a woman's desire for a child, and what a grace when this desire is embodied in a little one. The beginning of the journey starts with this first step: conception. A totally uncontrollable moment. The best planner can never decide for herself when that little being will nest in her womb. Even the new techniques cannot provide a success certificate or a guarantee of satisfaction, this moment when life is incarnated is in the hands of God alone.

From this union of bodies, from this intimacy filled with love, from this communion of body, heart and soul, comes life. There are, of course, much more painful cases, and I will talk about suffering in another chapter. There is the mourning, the child that does not come, or not at the right time, I understand all this. The announcement of a pregnancy can be a great surprise. As I said, the best organiser can never decide for herself when this little being will come to nest in her womb.

The heart of God is already revealing itself a little in this incarnation. I am one, me, my soul, my mind, my intelligence, my heart and my body. Many would like to control this body, to decide on the best time, the right situation, the ideal flat, a big car, a career change. What a temptation to think so much, to plan, to see with our human eyes what we think is best. Who has a bigger and more beautiful picture of the big picture of life? God of course, and God alone. I am not saying to welcome all children like a fool. Wisdom is a gift of the Spirit and some situations call for prudence or patience. On the other hand, life is in itself a treasure that cannot be controlled but is to be welcomed.

Welcoming something in my body that I cannot control is already a source of surrender. It is the first step in accepting that my soul and spirit, however eager for God, are quite helpless without grace.

For centuries, human beings have been hoping to dominate their bodies: we see this in diets, physical dictates that have evolved over the decades, excessive sport, certain forms of fasting that are fashionable today to dominate our bodies, to make them a tool in the service of our good intentions, our ideal. All this may be commendable, but it is simply human.

Disciplining my body is already a more accurate formulation. It avoids getting into a power struggle with my body, and it allows me to practice taking care of it, accepting it, knowing its limits so that I can acknowledge my humility. As a mother, there is also the dream pregnancy, the dream birth, the ideal baby (with hair, with rounded cheeks, with eyes of such and such a colour, with so many kilos, etc).

Sometimes gaining too much weight, having a difficult pregnancy or not experiencing the dream birth, sweet and delicious, is a real pain for the mother. Caesarean sections, forceps, hemorrhaging: all this is not a dream and reminds me that I don't have much control over my body.

The body is at the service of the soul. If my God became incarnate, if I believe in the Resurrection of the body, it is because the body has an inestimable value, it is the temple of the Spirit. So these limits, these weaknesses, what I may consider to be failures, are all means of bringing me back to humility, of allowing my intelligence to discover my weakness, of helping my spirit to accept my need for God, to recognise myself as a creature. These are all steps that help me to remember that I am only clay destined to be shaped in the loving hands of the potter. And I can assure you: the vase formed by His hands will be the most splendid to hold the most beautiful flowers, as long as the earth lets itself be shaped and worked. Trust in the skillful hands of the artist!

You may want to imagine the most beautiful vessel, the most ideal situation, the dream that would fill you, but start by trusting the Father. He will always find something more beautiful, more perfect and full of His infinite love than anything you could imagine with your human intelligence. Perhaps you will not see it right away, perhaps you will have to wait for His Glory to see God's plan with His own eyes, but be confident that He is preparing you for an eternity of happiness and praise.

Birth

After the potential inconveniences of pregnancy - some of which go off without a hitch - this little being comes to rest in my arms, turns its eyes towards me, seeks out my voice and my smell, likes to rest against me and listen to my heartbeat. What tenderness in these simple moments! Here is the first glimpse of the heart of God: a bath of infinite tenderness, a carnal union that passes through all the senses, a love that only asks to grow.

Like the newborn Jesus in the manger, you carry in your arms a newborn baby shaped by the hand of God. You have been the tabernacle of this new life. Without you having to do anything, life has become flesh. You become co-creator, your mother's heart united in the Father's heart.

From conception to birth, you make an image of Mary. She was visited by the angel who told her that Christ wanted to come into her and she said yes. By becoming a mother, Christ Himself wants to become incarnate in you. The heart of your child comes from the heart of God and is made in the image of His heart. By carrying a child, you are saying 'yes' to Christ who wants to reside in you. This is the first step, seemingly passive, since you are not literally in control. However, it requires a real choice, a decision, a "yes" on your part to welcome your little one, humble and vulnerable, in the image of our God, incarnate in our human condition and born in the cold of Christmas night.

Prayer of the Angelus

The Angel of the Lord declared to Mary :
And she conceived of the Holy Spirit.

Hail Mary...

Behold the handmaid of the Lord: Be it done unto me according to Thy word.

Hail May...

And the Word was made Flesh: And dwelt among us.

Hail Mary...

Pray for us, O Holy Mother of God, that we may be made worthy of the promises of Christ.

Let us pray:

Pour forth, we beseech Thee, O Lord, Thy grace into our hearts; that we, to whom the incarnation of Christ, Thy Son, was made known by the message of an angel, may by His Passion and Cross be brought to the glory of His Resurrection, through the same Christ Our Lord.

Amen

2-

Our children, love in relationship

Pitfalls of family life

Love grows with the pruning of the gardener. Do you dream of an ideal family, of well-behaved children who are good with friends, who share, of a household without shouting where everything goes well, of children who do their homework and excel in sports and music? The problem with this approach is that it relies on your own strengths. And you know it: "*Martha, Martha, you worry and fret about so many things...*" (Luke 10:41). By relying on your own strength, you will run out of steam... or even fall apart. In trying to build the ideal home with your own hands, you will fashion human ways, which may be very beautiful, but which will lose the divine aspect of your heart as a mother and your family life.

The family is the very image of God. The very image of the Trinity: one and three persons. One and Father, Son and

Holy Spirit. Your family is one, there are no two like yours, it is as unique as each of its members, even if you have identical twins (those who have lived with identical twins know that they are two very different people)!

I am convinced that the Father's heart is like the mother's heart: this heart gives everything, without holding anything back. This heart knows how to love despite the imperfections of its child. This heart has only one desire: the happiness of its little one. In my previous book "*Pause, and change your perspective",* I spoke about healthy authority: this authority filled with love that corrects in order to help people grow. The Father has all authority, Christ speaks with authority, but this authority is neither harsh nor violent, it does not point out error or sin. It is constantly lifting up, because this authority finds its foundation in love. By helping your children to grow up, you shape your heart into this authority full of tenderness, in the image of God.

Are you aware of the great mystery that dwells in your home? Are you aware of the absolute trust that the Lord has in you, entrusting you with his own children? Are you aware that the children in your home have only one vocation: to go and live in their Father's house?

But what do you do when your children are tiring or even unbearable, when the decibels get loud, when homework is sloppy, when the laundry is lying around or when some of

them come to blows rather than share heartily? There ⟩
much filial or brotherly love in such situations!

Let's go back to your mother's heart. What is it like a
these times? Agitated and hoping to get it over with quickly by
putting everyone to bed? Exasperated without the slightest
desire to listen to the conflict that is going on around the little
red car? Downhearted at the dishwasher that no one has had
the idea to empty? Depressed by the task that is resting on
your shoulders?

Stop for a moment. Remember: "*Come to me, all you
who labour and are overburdened, and I will give you rest*"
(Matthew 11:28).

Is it? Is it Christ who will empty the machine? Probably
not! But have you considered the possibility of Him being there
with you and giving you His peace? Have you considered that
He will give you His strength to carry out your daily task? Have
you considered that He gives you His joy to transform your
view of your children? Have you considered that He would give
you His very heart to love your children?

When Christ offers you to share his yoke, he does not
propose that you should be overwhelmed by trials with him,
quite the opposite! He offers you to come and carry your
humanity, to come to the rescue of your weakness. The yoke is
not there to imprison you to Him, but on the contrary to let
Him carry it for you! Check out the origin of the word and the

ᵛn the fields and countryside: the yoke on two

help each other, not to make one collapse

ᵣ the other!

ave you thought of calling Him? To ask Him for help in
ₙoments of discouragement and doubt? Just a phrase or
word you like, a word from a passage of the Word or a saint,
to catch His hand that is stretched out to you, to look at Him
who is always looking at you and is only waiting for you to look
up to Him.

At this moment you learn to act as a Child of God, to
live in the Spirit. Like your child who seeks your benevolent and
encouraging gaze before launching out. By placing yourself in
the hands of Christ, you taste his filial love for the Father. You
no longer rely on your own strength but on this divine love.
You learn to let God look at you. You learn to look at your
children and everyday situations with the very eyes of Christ.

If your children are tiring or even unbearable, step by
step, day after day, without dwelling on the past or worrying
about tomorrow, you will learn to make your heart available to
welcome their sadness or their anger. Like God's heart, your
heart will learn to welcome the being that is your child in
depth and in Truth at this moment of his life.

If the noise is unbearable, like God's heart, you will
teach them respect and silence, this sacred land that is the
other and that deserves to be taken care of.

If your children are greedy and fight for the biggest piece of cake, like God's heart, you will teach them to measure their food (this is already a first step to discover a simplified form of fasting), and you will teach them to control their desires. It was when Jesus was hungry in the desert that He rejected temptations. Do not take this aspect of family life lightly, it is one of the prisms for shaping a pure and strong soul in battle.

If homework is sloppy, like God's heart, you will be passing on the value of work and effort. You will teach your children that their vocation lies in developing their talents and being faithful to the gifts they have received. You will also teach them humility and courage when the task is difficult and their limitations become more evident.

If the laundry is lying on the floor, like God's heart, you will teach them the meaning of service. Christ himself became a servant and humbled himself. Growing in dedication to others involves small actions such as remembering to put their laundry in the basin, empty the dishwasher or clear their place at the table, or perhaps even their place and that of their neighbour! Gently teach your children to go a little further than what they think is the limit of their love!

If your children refuse to share, like God's heart, take the time to stop, to get down on your knees, physically on their level, to show them how reaching out to their brother or sister is good, is a Good. If your child feels loved with an unlimited love, if they know they have an irreplaceable place in the family, if they trust your love, they will learn to seek the strength and dedication to give. I would advise against forcing a child to do a good deed against his will: done against his will, this so-called good deed could create resentment in the siblings. Rather than being the judge of the conflict, act as a guide to steer them onto a path of kindness and love. This will take time, but it is the first characteristic of love according to St Paul: "*Love is patient*" (first letter to the Corinthians).

Patience is not a passive quality: it requires perseverance and endurance, it is a way of learning to respond rather than react. The key to learning patience is to ask the Lord to increase our Faith, the Faith that our children are the way the Lord has chosen to bring us closer to Him.

Always and unceasingly, in the image of the heart of God, your heart as a mother will help the hearts of your children to expand to welcome the other. Christ taught us: "*Love one another as I have loved you*" (John 15:12).

Here is your family in the hands of the Father, nourished by the example of Christ and united in the Holy Spirit. The Holy Spirit who unites each member of the family, that love which uplifts and comforts, which rejoices, which gives advice, which invites prudence, which guides, which softens. All forms of brotherly love find their source in the Holy Spirit.

Sins and virtues

The Church has given us the seven deadly sins to keep us alert in the fight. Armed with this knowledge, we can ensure that we and our children are committed to the virtues opposing these sins.

A good way to grow and let grace work in us is to make sure we choose virtue. Fighting sin, yes, but if we focus on it and on our own strength to stifle it, we will weaken. Let us not keep our minds fixed on our sins or those of our children: by grace, Peter walked on the waters because he kept his eyes fixed on Jesus. The moment he thinks about his condition, he sinks! In the same way, let us not look at sin all the time, it gives the enemy too much pleasure. Let us be aware of it, so that we may return unceasingly to Mercy - we will speak of the sacraments later - but let us keep our gaze fixed on Christ and the virtues of His heart.

Below is my summary of the book "Les sept péchés capitaux" by Pascal Ide (éditions Mame):

Sins

Pride - *captain of the deadly sins*
Self-love, importance of others' gaze, self-satisfaction, vanity in small achievements, perfectionism, disdain, arrogance, selfishness (living for oneself), independence (living for oneself), sulking, refusal of criticism

Gluttony - *not the most serious but the most accessible*
Immoderate pleasure, gluttony over the quality of the food, over the time (getting ahead of the meal), over the manner (lacking propriety and politeness), spiritual gluttony, gossip, backbiting, exuberance, lack of control, negligence

Lust - *hurts the other, oneself and God*
In the imagination, through the eyes, through words that reduce the other to mere desire, masturbation, relationships outside marriage

Greed - *inordinate love of possessions*
Taste for money, furniture, clothes, trinkets, books, being stingy with one's time, stingy with services rendered, fear of giving, wish to have more, worry about the future

Envy, jealousy - *sin against others and against oneself*
Sadness about what the other has, what the other is, lack of self-esteem, denial of God's Love which gives what it wants to each person, malice, satisfaction with the difficulties of others, resentment, critical spirit, difficulty in trusting, dispersion in one's activities

Anger - *offence against others, and against God who intended diversity [however, there is healthy anger = right object, right intention, measured reaction].*

Desire for revenge, taking justice into one's own hands, disappointment in another who reacts differently from oneself, anger against oneself, anger against God in trials

Laziness and acedia - *a sin especially of the mature age, the midday demon*

Sadness of soul, spiritual languor, lack of taste for prayer, arid interior life, disgust for action, putting off until tomorrow, seeking palliatives to one's boredom, restlessness in order to avoid facing God, inconstancy, lack of firmness in one's resolutions, impatience to see results, excessive taste for relaxation

The opposing virtues

Pride ----- practice **humility**

Accepting humiliation and acknowledging one's part of the truth, giving of one's time, heart and skills, accepting to be bound, giving a smile, a look, a presence, cultivating discretion (less use of 'I' and 'me'), stopping self-control, accepting one's moods, seeing all things as coming from the hand of God, avoiding false modesty, accepting one's talents as gifts, acknowledging one's debts, thanking those who support us, blessing and speaking well of others

Gluttony ----- **self-control, renunciation**

Integrate desire but renounce excesses, listen to the needs of the body more than to pleasure, thank God for food, know how to renounce, treat the cause (I eat out of boredom => go for a walk, read a book, listen to music...)

*Lust ----- cultivating **chastity***
To seek bodily and spiritual unity, to see the beauty of sexuality, to revisit one's motives, to commit one's will, to preserve one's gaze, to watch one's speech, to purify one's imagination and curiosity, to accept one's weakness, to confess one's faults in spite of one's shame, to ask God for this virtue

*Greed ----- practise **sobriety and generosity***
Do not neglect this vice, give thanks to God for your possessions, practice sobriety and trust, be generous, give away what you no longer use, set a portion of your budget for the Lord

*Envy ----- **blessing** the other and cultivating **self-esteem***
Accepting the other without criticizing or accusing, not avoiding the person you jealously, accepting the lack, reasoning with yourself, cultivating your self-esteem, choosing to bless

*Anger ----- cultivating **patience and gentleness***
Step back, be silent while anger passes, but don't run away, say things, settle the conflict and make peace, put yourself in the other person's shoes, practice gentleness, practice humility, de-idealise, give up perfectionism, limit stimulants, forgive

*Laziness ----- keep **joy**, use **perseverance***
Living in the present moment, living as a child of God, thirsting for His presence, persevering in prayer and in one's

duties as a state, weeping over one's sadness in order to be consoled, humbly accepting one's misery, sleeping according to one's personal needs (but not more), acting by prioritising one's tasks, taking initiatives

What a programme! We can draw on these resources to make progress. Not to climb an inaccessible and discouraging mountain, but to leave the door open to God's love, and close the skylight left open to the enemy.

Our sins need to be pierced with the arrows of the Father to be broken. In suffering or difficulty, let us ask for Faith, to believe that God is at work to purify us. Let us implore Mary, Mother of God and Mother of Mercy to protect us with her maternal mantle. Her mantle is the Holy Spirit himself! *"The Holy Spirit will come upon you, and the power of the Most High will cover you with its shadow"* (Luke 1:35): yes, this mantle is the Holy Spirit! *"He will lead you to the complete Truth"* (John 16:13).

Prayer and action

Focus on 'being' and not on 'doing'. You will always have a thousand things to do. Keep in mind that being must always come first. Learn to stop, to give your time, to lie down on the floor to draw with your children, to ride the train with them, to play a board game, to ask about the good moments of their day (not only the academic aspects but also about their table mate in the canteen or which friend made a good joke!)

Today's society calculates in efficiency. What efficiency is there in what I have just listed? None: just pure love. You need time for yourself, your children need time for themselves, and you need time together. This is where the relationship is created, where the knowledge of the other begins.

Wouldn't you consider marrying someone you've never spent time with? Good for you! This applies to time spent with your children... and to time spent in heart-to-heart prayer with the Lord. But we'll talk about prayer later.

Remember that the love you give your children is the prism through which they will perceive God's love. Are you bossy, do you have difficulty listening or giving your time, patience and tenderness? Your children may be reluctant to surrender to God. Are you trying to be gentle, kind and caring? Your children will be confident that God's heart is wonderful: like Mum's, but even more beautiful and bigger!

Do you hope to nourish and strengthen their souls so that they will indeed have the gift of Faith? There is only one way: pray for them and ask for the Holy Spirit for yourself.

St. Therese of Lisieux Jesus wrote: "*We must always pray as if action were useless and act as if prayer were insufficient.*" Pray and give tenderness, gentleness, listening, comfort in all things. This is the key to a united family.

I could also be considered demanding in my education. This is true, but it is out of love. Christ is also demanding: He asks for our whole life, our soul, our heart and our body. I hope I am not demanding like a tyrant: love must always come first. But as a mother, I am also here to raise my children and guide them towards a greater love. The aim is never to make them despair, to discourage their enthusiasm. Each child must be convinced that they are worthy of being loved as they are, and that they are indeed fully loved. It was a great wound in my childhood to have this feeling of never "being or doing good enough". May the Lord be blessed for this wound that has allowed me to walk in order to present myself before Him as I am, to know that I am totally loved exactly as I am, no matter how beautiful or miserable I am on this day.

The unity of the siblings comes from this aspect: learning to love the other as he is. I was talking about shouting: of course, we must avoid shouting. I was talking about respect: of course, we must not hit, and we must know how to say stop when a child is violent with us. Without aggression, but by setting the limits of our physical, personal and spiritual space. The limits set must be simple and clear, firmly defined. We are holy land. Everyone is holy land.

Children also learn to love with a greater love. It is easy to love your brother or sister when they share your books, it becomes much harder when one yells at the other. As a mother, I can show the one who has been hurt that yes, the situation is unfair and that he or she has not done anything, that maybe the other one is yelling because he or she is hurting inside (for example, because his or her best friend left school or a classmate hurt him or her today, or his or her new pen was broken, or he or she lost the football game). This does not excuse the unfortunate behaviour, but it does make it possible to forgive, and to accept the other, however miserable he or she may be. So forgiveness creates a true union of hearts. And what an immense gift it is to know that family supports us even when we have fallen. That our family is there to pick us up and walk with us, as Christ himself does with His Church.

Do not hesitate to read the lives of the saints you love, to pray to the patron saints of your family, to discover new writings of the prophets of all times. Their intercession is powerful: they are already in the Glory of God, and the enemy cannot approach your family when you speak of the beauties of Creation, the saints and the Glory of the Kingdom of God.

So arm yourself with gentleness and patience, you can't imagine the power of these two virtues. They are the first step to living goodness and joy in your family and spreading them around you. Gentleness and patience shape the heart from within, the innermost part of your soul. Then Christ Himself will give you the strength to follow Him and use His virtues to radiate around you. You will be able to bear many fruits, the fruits of God, those fruits that He wants to give to the world in order to attract all souls to Him.

Beware of imagination and interpretation

They are tools of choice for the enemy who makes you imagine the worst, regret the past or fear the future. Interpretation, too, which invites you to judge your own heart as well as the hearts of others, whereas God alone knows the intimacy of your soul. He himself knows you better than you know yourself. You must fight firmly against these two points.

Invite Truth and clarity into your story. Bring to light your false beliefs, interpretations, projections. This healthy - and holy! - light allows you to remove the shadows that damage your heart and pollute your story.

Freed from these two pitfalls, you become free to follow the plan the Father has for your life. It may be a daily renunciation, but stand firm in the Faith to believe the Truth, to live in the Spirit of Truth.

The lie always comes from the enemy, the Prince of lies. You will be confronted with the lies of the world, it is up to you to watch and stand firm and armed in this discernment between the way of the world and the way of God. Imagination and interpretation are two lies that lie in your own heart: you have the hand to clean up your story. This is the way to read your story in Truth and move forward in freedom.

3-

Ask for Faith

In my family, I often heard mockery of Thomas, who did not even believe in the Resurrection of Christ. Thomas needed God's mercy to make his faith firm. What a gift he received through his blessed doubt! Jesus loved him so much that he allowed him to put his hand in his side, in the very source of his Mercy. So Thomas believes. Mercy is the source of the gift of Faith. A firm and unshakeable Faith. No more doubt, no more questioning, no more verification that God is the Almighty at work in his history.

I received the grace of Thomas. A complete healing of all my wounds, and even visible proof of it. This healing is a pure gift, a pure grace of pure love. This healing is not a conclusion or a reward, but the first step to follow Christ in a new way, through the intercession of my dear mother in Heaven. Life is a journey, I am always on the move and the treasures in my story are many pearls to make my faith grow, so many gifts from the Father to make me come back to Him.

By remaining on the vine, you too bear the fruit of God the Father. Cling to Christ, he will give you his own fruit. The pruning is painful, his word is demanding, unquestioning, and sometimes even sharp. But the key is always love.

Christ gives you Faith, Hope and Charity. Paul says that, of all these, the greatest virtue is Charity. Right, Love is the key. Note also that of all these, the first in the list is Faith. Hope and Charity flow from Faith. Then your Charity will be transformed. Faith is the most important because it transfigures all things. So begin by asking for Faith. Faith can move mountains, it changes everything. And you know that if you ask your Father in Heaven for it, He will not refuse you such a gift, because He created you to live in His heart. If you ask for a red car or a bigger flat, perhaps you will have to wait, especially if it does not correspond to His will, if it is not a source of Good for you. He knows. But ask for Faith, persevere, persevere in your request. Christ comes to meet you at the well of the Samaritan woman, Jacob's well, so deep like the depth of the prophets' Faith.

Ask for Faith for your children too. You will see that the simplicity, the purity, the innocence of their hearts, of their living Faith will show you the way to Christ. Entrust your heart, that of your spouse and that of your children to Mary. You will learn step by step, throughout your life, to love Jesus with a mother's heart, and to return unceasingly to the Father's house.

4-

Prayer and spiritual warfare

Praying as a family

It is through prayer that the Lord can come to dwell in your heart. Beware, the lurking enemy will not let you rest and will not let you preserve this time so easily: tiredness, family organisation, journeys, stewardship, hunger or thirst, an urgent email... The enemy can use a thousand strategies to make this heart-to-heart time with God take second place to the human tasks of our state duty. However, prayer is the source for the human tasks of our state duty to be accomplished in the heart of God.

Teach your children to pray, guide them to meet Christ, He too was a newborn and a child, like them. You fed your children when they were infants, do not forget when they grow up, to continue to feed their souls.

It starts with prayer at home, prayer as a family. Even a child who cannot yet speak should be part of this time, the ultimate moment when the Lord sits in the midst of your family, looking down with love and tenderness on each member.

You will have to be creative: candles, yes, if the children are not too small, one candle per child to avoid the battle of who will blow out. One day read the Word, one day say a dozen rosaries, one day pray an 'Our Father' and share intentions. You can have a fixed structure, you are also free to renew this time when prayer becomes difficult. Family prayer is not a straitjacket or an obligation but a place of living relationship with Christ. If no one has the heart to pray, accept your smallness, keep it short and simple, but remain faithful to this daily appointment. Children love to discover new things, it's their age! Take advantage of their wonder to sow the joy of knowing the living Word, the gushing Source.

By varying the ways in which they talk to Jesus, children also discover which conversation they prefer. Just as you offer them different vegetables to form their taste, so form their taste for prayer! This is the greatest gift you can give them in life, the only thing that will keep them confident in the boat with Jesus throughout their lives, whatever the waves and winds.

The 'Our Father' and the 'Hail Mary' are probably the basis. The Act of Contrition and the Creed as they grow up.

Don't forget to read the Word. There are materials suitable for all ages: comics, illustrated Bible. My advice would be to try to use a medium that respects the exact words of the Bible. These are the words of Christ himself for each of us. Again, be creative: read the gospel of the day, or in the morning the refrain of the psalm at lauds, or in the evening the prayer at compline. The Word is rich, you will never exhaust the possibilities, the messages, the styles, the stories. God wants to speak to us again and again; his Word is even richer than Jacob's deep well!

Gently invite them to silent prayer. This heart to heart is so privileged where Jesus can come and rest in your heart. Children have a heart that is particularly willing to let Jesus in, and Jesus loves to see them come to Him. This prayer is sometimes little known, or neglected. The word 'silent prayer' in itself can be discouraging. It is not easy to keep time and silence for God: it is so much easier to fill it with a thousand activities and a thousand speeches, especially in our so connected society. However, when you teach your children silence, their ears open, as on the day of their baptism, and God's graces flood them with his love.

In silent prayer, imitate their childlike heart. If the Lord has given you the blessing of being a mother, it is to bring you closer to Him. Your children can show you the way to God's heart in many ways. So sit down, explain to them that you are going to keep a time of silence to listen to God, that they probably won't hear anything with their ears, but that nevertheless they can have Faith, believe deeply that Christ is there in their hearts, that he will inspire them with his Holy Spirit, now or later in the day. When I am silent, when I quiet the restlessness of my heart, when I seek to hear the gentle breeze, then the Lord himself teaches me, shapes me, watches me, guides me, loves me.

It doesn't matter if one of the children is watching the timer for the three minutes of silent prayer we agreed on together, it doesn't matter if two of them start to giggle, if they don't stand perfectly still, we're not here to play musical statues. Remember that Jesus loves your children far more than you love them, so bring them to Him, put them in His lap.

Keep in mind that the hearts of children have a simplicity and innocence that is good soil for the seed sown by Christ to grow. The seed will germinate in its own time, and if you have had the grace to begin in early childhood to share this prayer as a family, persevere, do not be discouraged. Beautiful fruits are being prepared. And it is never too late to come to family prayer! It's just that, as we get older, there are sometimes more barriers - fears, bashfulness, false beliefs - to be broken down in order to present ourselves, as individuals and as a family, before God, as we are. Never despair of what the Lord can prepare for your child: your ways are not His ways.

Think also that your children see you praying. When they see you happy in your heart-to-heart with God, on your knees, still, focused on this time of intimacy with God and not on the temptation to be the policeman, even if they move, laugh or slip a joke to the person next to them, they will feel that this time takes priority over everything else.

I remember a time of prayer during which my children were rather quiet, but as I wrote it down, I smiled inwardly at the little laughter I heard around me. What a joy this living prayer is! I prefer a few muffled laughs to a grumpy silence. Maybe they were moving, but not excessively so, because with my eyes closed I didn't mind. When I opened my eyes again when the timer went off, confirmed by one of the children, who kept saying "beep beep", one of my children looked at me, we exchanged a smile and this child gave me a kiss. What tenderness in that look. I don't know what happened in his heart, what he perceived from my prayer or from God himself, it will remain in the intimacy of his heart and soul and I don't need to ask for explanations, but these times of prayer also teach you to see the Lord at work, to perceive that, at times, the Grace is there, very real and very tangible. For a few moments, a deep communion that needs no words settles in your home.

So don't judge your prayer time or that of your children. The Lord's ways are not our ways, only He knows what He puts in their hearts and souls. What you can be sure of is that all the time you spend praying, sharing the bread of his Word, adoring the Blessed Sacrament, going to meet Jesus in the Host at Mass, all these times are moments of great blessings, times when you leave time to reach eternity. It is Heaven begun in the midst of your family.

Persevere even if you do not see the fruits. Love is exercised in faithfulness. You know this well as a wife. Persevere, be on time, teach your children to make themselves available for Christ. Have complete confidence in God that this time offered for Him is a blessed time that expands your heart and that of your children. The very heart of your family expands to radiate with the very love of God and bear its fruit.

The need for a good spiritual director

Your mother's soul needs a guide. First of all, you have the Lord of course. Then you have your husband, he is the guardian of your soul and your family. I also advise you to have a good spiritual director. Not "good" in the sense of competent, reliable, but the right spiritual director for you. For this, pray to the Lord to guide you towards the priest, the nun, the person who will allow you to shed light on your soul, your heart, your decisions, the events in your life history. With his help, you will avoid your own biases, tame your imagination and put an end to your abusive interpretation. By putting words to your life, you will tell your story in Truth.

Pray a lot before asking the person you think is good for you. The special thing about a spiritual father is that he is chosen by his child. It is not the father who chooses his child. It's the opposite of you welcoming your children: your children have not chosen you, it's the Father who has chosen you as parents for them. This is different, it is up to you to take the step. Discern, therefore, to ask the person according to the ways of the Lord, not according to your human desires. The Lord takes care of everything, He will know how to correct your aim if you do not direct yourself towards the right person: His will will be done, as long as you ask Him to guide you in His way.

You will have a spiritual director who will help you to see God's work in your life, your children's life, your family's life. As busy mums, we can be quick to worry about anything that could be improved, whether it's in the organisation or expectations of each other, in daily life or in holiday plans. The enemy excels at making Hope flinch.

A good spiritual director helps to bring to light God's action in our lives. It gives great impetus and support to live with Faith, Hope and Charity. It will help you name the temptations and you will see that the enemy hates to be named and looked at in the open! No matter how hard it is, no matter what the trials are, you will move forward with a heart that is confident that God will take care of everything.

Three stages of prayer

There are stages in the life of Faith. Many mystics have written about this. If I stick to a simple mummy approach, there is a first level where we ask for what we need: that the baby sleeps, that the teacher understands our child, that friends are nice, that the exam goes well, that our child gets into this school, that the baby arrives when I get my promotion or when we find our dream flat.

This step is good and necessary: Jesus said to pray to our Father who listens to his children and responds to their needs. We have a perfect Father in Heaven and it is good to turn to Him, to think of Him, to ask. However, let us not stop there.

Then there are two options: either we are heard and we are happy, but this state is fragile. Indeed, if we are not answered, we risk thinking that the Lord is hard, that the Father is not so good, or that He is a judge who waits for us to do "better" before granting our request. We doubt His unconditional love, His goodness, we think we have to earn His grace by dint of our achievements and dedication. All this is pure temptation from the enemy and it is easy to get caught up in the banana peel he slips under our feet. This is the whole story of original sin and the temptation to doubt a love that wants our happiness! So it's time to choose the third option.

This third option begins with a decision: to decide to pray with all our heart, but always keeping in mind and first of all that "*Your will be done, not mine*" (Luke 22:42) because the Father knows well what is good for us and what He is preparing for us. Sometimes we will need patience and trust. In a word, we will have to love before anything else. But isn't that our attitude as mothers? If our child asks us for a sweet just before the meal when we have just prepared a delicious dish and a tasty dessert, we will refuse by telling him to wait a few more minutes, that the meal is almost ready and that he will enjoy it. Our Father acts with the same impulse as our mother's heart. This total trust in God's will is the beginning of holiness.

There is a final step that comes only through grace. Once we have decided to trust the Father's will in all things, only grace works in our lives. We can pray to hasten the coming of grace, but only the Lord knows and decides when He will come to rest in us. This is a new stage of sanctification of our life. Then our life radiates with the joy and sweet warmth of the Father's love. We become that lamp that illuminates souls with the light of God, we become that salt that delicately enhances the taste in the history of the people that the Lord puts on our path. We begin to love our children with the very heart of Christ and His Mother and we become an instrument of sanctification for our children. What a grace! God the Father calls all mothers to this holiness, because the love present in the heart of a family is the image of Trinitarian love: one family, one father, one mother, children, one pure love that unites each of the members, each one being unique and wonderful.

Beware, the aim is not to climb as many rungs as possible, the life of Faith is not a race but a seed that grows every day, according to the sun, the clouds and the rain. Let us invite the Lord to our family table, and let us be taken where Christ wishes, in the Spirit, for the greater Glory of the Father.

5-

Suffering

Suffering in everyday life

Mothers know so well that suffering is part of life, from the illness of a little one, to the wickedness of the world, to wounds that are intentional or caused by clumsiness. When we become mothers, suffering becomes more profound: how wonderful it would be to prevent our children's hearts from suffering! To spare them from sadness and tears! The good news is that this time will come: "*He will wipe away all tears from their eyes; there will be no more death, and no more mourning or sadness. The world of the past has gone.*" Revelation 21:4). "*Look towards him and be radiant; let your faces not be abashed.*" as Psalm 33:6 says.

So when you are upset about something, offer it to the Lord for all the families in the same situation. This is the communion of saints: the intercession of one saves many souls. You are called to holiness and to this same communion to bring many souls back to the heart of God.

Your superior bypasses you and puts his name in place of yours on the presentation of that project you have been working on for six months? Offer up to Jesus all the lying souls who are in particular need of his mercy. However, it will surely be good to talk to your boss face to face to put into words and clarify what has happened. There is no need for value judgements, accusations or verbal abuse that would prevent the person you are talking to from listening to the heart of what you are saying, but show objectively what has happened in order to help everyone grow.

"*Did you take my name off? I worked on this project for six months.*" And that's it. You will see the answer, if there is one. With the grace of the Spirit, everyone will be edified and grow through this event.

Do you feel left out and rejected in your family? Offer to Jesus all the suffering hearts in the name of His Name, who was rejected to the point of dying on a cross.

Has someone, perhaps even your child, betrayed your trust? Offer this suffering to Jesus, who was abandoned by all his friends in Gethsemane (except John). Remember that Jesus forgave up to that point. At the Resurrection, Christ does not reproach Peter for having betrayed him, even though He had warned him, out of love, to show him that He is loved beyond his misery. It is a gift from Christ to prevent Peter from despairing of himself and to make him taste His infinite Mercy. With this example, ask Christ for His Peace and forgive those who have betrayed you. Your children have to learn the crucial aspect of truth and the disasters of lies, but gentleness, patience and delicacy, like Christ towards Peter, are the way for you to love them beyond their miseries.

You arrive at Mass and a friend ignores you or doesn't see you? Offer to Jesus all the families who are not there today, ignore Him or do not see Him. Your annoyance or hurt will become a gift to comfort the heart of Christ.

In all things, pray not to hold grudges, desires for revenge or bitterness. Pacify your heart by regular confession. Mercy alone is the source of true peace. Christ dreams of carrying you in His arms. The more you surrender, the more your Father carries you in His arms. You know as a mother, it is easier to carry and rock a sleeping or relaxed child in your arms, than a child who is gesticulating to get down. Like children, remain calm and peaceful, surrendered to the arms of your heavenly Father.

Concretely, what is the offering of our suffering?

I am talking about offering your suffering, but perhaps you are wondering what this means in practice?

The offering of your suffering is above all an invitation from Christ. It is in no way a matter of wallowing in suffering.

49

By reasoning in this way, by seeking suffering, you are not in the Father's hands full of goodness. You will know in the depths of your soul whether you are in an attitude of complacency or in front of an invitation. If need be, describe the situation on paper, write down words detailing the situation: you will see objectively if you are overdoing it or not. If you are accusing, judging, angry, bitter: your heart is not at peace and you are not being invited. You are facing a wound, but not an invitation to offer your suffering.

Suffering is an invitation: Christ presents you with a cup and invites you to follow Him. "*Come, follow me*". I have not counted the number of times these words are spoken in the Bible, they are the words that Christ wants to say to everyone because He is thirsty for us, thirsty for our love for Him. You see this suffering, and then you make a decision: to follow Christ today or not. Do not despair of yourself, some days you may say "no", but the more you taste these invitations, the more you will savour the meal offered.

I repeat: do not seek suffering, but wait for the invitation. Christ is the shepherd who guides you, in his time and in his grace. Do not force grace or suffering.

A strong temptation from the enemy in the face of this invitation will be to make you fear the worst. If I offer the suffering of my supervisor given as an example above, will always be treated like the last wheel in the carriage? If I offer the suffering of rejection from someone close to me, will always be humiliated or rejected? If I forgive someone who has betrayed me, will they not do it again? Do I see myself as weak?

Remember that you have refused to indulge in these situations, so in Truth you are not seeking them. It is not your attitude or your state of mind that initiates these sufferings. You are not a doormat but a mother invited to let her inner strength grow! So, if you are well in front of an invitation, the temptation to fear the worst is the enemy's solution to make you say "no".

I have often smiled to myself at such an invitation, fearing that I would suffer all day from such an event... when it lasted only a few minutes! I am so little that the Lord asks me to follow Him and offers me His cup in XXS version for a few moments. He is quite right, so limited I could not bear more!

Do not be afraid, Christ is preparing you, shaping you. The Father takes care of the beautiful seed of your life and helps your soul to grow and bear His fruit. By answering "yes" to this invitation, you join Christ in His Eucharistic sacrifice. Yes, yes, nothing less! The Latin origin of the word "sacrifice" is not at all negative: sacrificium means "to make sacred"! You discover a new dimension of the cross: the joy of the blessed!

The certainty that you are indeed in the offering of yourself, in the union of your suffering with the sufferings of Christ, is joy! We will talk more about this later. Your suffering in an offering process is painful in the depths of your soul. It is not something that you share and bring to light to anyone who wants to know. You would be there in complacency and pride, in false humility.

The suffering offered is painful, really painful, in your soul, your heart or your body. Sometimes all three. But there is no despair because you have full confidence that this cross for you is a way of salvation for your soul and many others!

The suffering ends, so you can look at this ordeal and say, "I have suffered". It may be at the threshold of your life that this suffering ends, but it does have an end. Suffering is a passage, it is not the finish. The arrival of the path is the Glory of the Resurrection. This "I have suffered" takes on the dimension of eternity and bears much fruit.

You do not have to seek these sufferings, but Christ, in gratitude for accepting his invitation, will make you taste his own Glory, the jubilation of the blessed. It will begin with very small things, but love begins there, as your mother's heart knows. Look at your children's first drawings, so clumsy and touching. In the Father's heart, you are that child, clumsy but so touching because of your good will.

You see it too when you see a child making a real effort to share, to forgive his brother for the brand new toy he has just broken, for a smile of gratitude when you have comforted him. You are that child in the Father's heart. There is no smal drama or "it doesn't matter", neither for a pain in the life of your children, nor for your heart as a mother who gives herself out of love, without holding anything back for herself.

Suffering has value, if it is lived in Love. You would not say of the cross that "it is not serious, because there is the Resurrection". In the family too, recognise the moments of suffering. Do not let the enemy appropriate suffering and leave only bitterness or resentment. Your suffering too has value in the heart of God, the sufferings of your children too have value in the heart of God, as long as Love remains at the centre.

The suffering of Christ

Our God became incarnate out of love for us, to save us and give us eternal life. For this he suffered. What a mystery the cross is. Our mother's heart is a privileged place to understand the mystery of the cross and to live from it.

You've probably experienced it: your three-year-old, proud to discover his abilities and take on new challenges, climbs high and waves at you. You see him wobble, your stomach clenches, your whole body freezes, your blood runs cold and you break out in a cold sweat... Phew, he's caught himself and you invite him to start his descent with care. This example shows how deeply your love is rooted in your flesh.

The Father's love became incarnate in Jesus Christ. The Father also loves us with this love anchored in the flesh, He who gave us His own Son. How did He love? What was the path chosen? Not the glory of a great king born in a palace, riding into Jerusalem on a great white steed and freeing his people from the oppressor. No. He was born in a stable, entering Jerusalem on a colt and freeing us from sin through the cross.

Many 'whys' are born in suffering: Why me? Why now? Why the illness? Why death? And a mother's heart is so sensitive to suffering: how painful it is to see your child suffer. How painful it is that a child rejects us and makes us suffer.

I would be tempted to say that, fortunately, the previous chapter has shown you how the relationship with your children shapes this divine love in your heart and in the heart of your family. You have seen how your heart becomes the temple of God's own love. So yes, suffering will probably find its way into your heart, because before that eternity of Glory, there is the cross. But note that this chapter is placed, as in your life, between the discovery of this love in relationship, and joy. True joy. The joy that no one on earth and no suffering can take away from you. We will come to that.

I shared earlier that the offering of suffering begins in small ways. I can see in my story through my journey, God's grace at work to draw me ever more to Him, in my reactions to events, and in the sufferings and pains of life.

The first time I carried my floppy toddler in my arms, thinking he was dead, I prayed "*No Lord, not that*". The Lord was very good to me in taking that cup away from me.

Then, when the doctors couldn't find the cause of my child's condition, I prayed, in tears, saying, "*Lord, if You want to bring him back to You now, OK, but You'd better help me because I can't do it alone.*" Blessed be the Lord for my child back home.

When I had the immense joy of being pregnant with a little one, when I experienced the immense joy of carrying the first moments of life, and when I suddenly understood that soon this little life would no longer be inside my womb, I prayed and sobbed: "*My baby, if the Father calls you back now, go, go peacefully, you can be at peace, we will meet again.*

How I will miss you." A pain without words that many of you know. A new step to look more often to Heaven through the intimate union with our children already resting in the Glory of the Father. To begin to guess the communion of saints, our glorious bodies united in an eternity of love.

Suffering changes the intimacy of our souls, our hearts and our bodies as mothers. For me, the Mass has become the perfect place to be in communion with my child, a moment of eternity during which the whole heavenly community exults and praises God, with me here on earth receiving Jesus in the Host and my little one praising the Father's wonders in Heaven: at this moment, we are even more united than we have been able to experience during these times of incarnate life. It is a foretaste of the Heaven that I will taste in eternity.

Sometimes the suffering is so heavy, the sadness so intense, that it is difficult not to despair. But Christ is always there to go before us and to lift us up. Suffering also allows us to put the essential first in our lives, to rediscover the perspective of eternity, to decide once again to put love first, to return to the sacraments.

Our Lady is our example of faith, trust and love: at the foot of the cross her heart was pierced, yet she believed, she knew what her Son, who is also her God, was doing. Unite your heart with Mary's to learn the meaning of the cross. Christ desires our salvation.

Mary always guides us to her Son, who is the Way, the Truth and the Life. He is the door to our Father's house. Asking Mary to take us under her mantle, that is to say, to protect us by the Holy Spirit who herself took her under his shadow, let us ask her to guide us towards the Mass, towards the most total union with her Son in the Eucharist. From being co-creators (as I shared with you in the chapter from 'Conception to Birth'), we become co-redemptresses: united to the wounds of Christ, we present our children to the Father, but also all the children of the earth. We become the heart that makes it possible to bring as many souls as possible to the Father's house.

Rather than looking for answers to our "whys", suffering is soothed in surrender. This does not mean that our emotions will be anaesthetised or erased! Our suffering would even lose its value if all emotion were erased. Our suffering has meaning because it is real, and Christ will teach us to accept it without despair, to share His cross.

I am not talking about the cross as a gift. I am talking about an invitation to follow Christ in suffering and share His cross. The cross is not a gift, a goal. The cross is a scandal. Yes, the scandal of the cross! But the Father transfigures all crosses offered out of love. It is the Father who transfigured his Son "[Jesus] was transfigured", Matthew 17:2). It is the Father who raised his Son ("[Jesus] is not here; he has risen", Luke 24:6). It is the Glory of the Father, of the Son glorified in the Father, it is the great victory over evil. The cross is an invitation to a greater love, a love that goes beyond human limits.

The Resurrection does not diminish the suffering of the cross, nor does it erase the marks of the Passion, but your life, united to the wounds of Christ, is transfigured with Him. You begin to live by the Spirit. And this is the path of a whole life.

Your suffering is salvific because you die to yourself to be reborn of the Spirit. Is this not clear? The key is always Love.

If you leave in the morning convinced that your child is going to get hurt, and in the evening the teacher tells you that your child has fallen, do not think that you have foreknowledge. Only God has complete and true knowledge. On the other hand, would you not have invited the enemy to your breakfast table? By these thoughts, have you not left the door open for his evil deeds? A good spiritual director or a holy priest can help you to see, with God's grace.

Suffering is salvific when it is lived and accepted out of love. Not sought or chosen, but accepted. Not out of masochism or because you should suffer for some reason! God wants your happiness! Your true happiness. Your total exultation in Him. He wants you to put your spirit into His hands. It is the enemy who whispers that all this is not real or that you should suffer for this or that reason. There is no other reason than Love.

If the Lord allows a cross in your life, you can be sure that He has a plan. You can have full confidence that this willing trial will draw you to Him and offer you - in His time - a greater happiness, a more beautiful room in the Father's house. Follow Christ without fear. In His heart you can rest in peace. In His hands you are unshakeable. Your mother's heart in God's heart, your joy is perfect.

What better intercessor than Mary his mother, whose heart is totally united with that of her divine Son? Ask her for her own heart to love her Son, and she will take you tenderly in her arms, close to her divine child. And Jesus himself will take you with him to his Father.

Memorare

Remember, O most gracious Virgin Mary, that never was it known that anyone who fled to thy protection, implored thy help, or sought thine intercession was left unaided.

Inspired by this confidence, I fly unto thee, O Virgin of virgins, my mother; to thee do I come, before thee I stand, sinful and sorrowful.

O Mother of the Word Incarnate, despise not my petitions, but in thy mercy hear and answer me.

Amen

6-

The domestic church

The sacraments

In our first steps towards our Father, the enemy acts with great fanfare. The events that try to hinder our journey are clear enough, if we take the time to look at our history. When we begin to find the Peace of God, the enemy must use more subtle feints. We must learn to sharpen our minds, to ask for the light of the Holy Spirit so that we do not fall into these traps. This is the path of a lifetime, it is also the struggle of each day. But let us not fear, Christ has already defeated evil, the Virgin has already crushed the head of the serpent.

To build a strong domestic church, let us lay the right bricks: the sacraments:

Baptism: Children and parents are children of God. We must have great respect for our children because parents are not to dominate them but to educate them. Parents are to love their children and guide them to grow upright and bear fruit. The Lord has entrusted us with children to bring them to holiness. We have a very important authority to exercise, but in no way to dominate. Our parental and spiritual authority must always be at the service of our children's love. Let us watch our words, our actions and our decisions, let us discern our motives and the Spirit that directs us each day.

Confession: This delightful sacrament is the source of forgiveness and mercy. We can do no good without recourse to this sacrament. Reconciliation with the Father restores us to our integrity as children of God when we have severed our bond with him. The Father has infinite patience with us. As a family, let us return to Him again and again with sincere contrition. This sacrament is the source of forgiveness shared in the family, and a happy family needs to know how to forgive, a happy family needs to learn not to cultivate resentment, the spirit of revenge or bitterness. Forgiveness allows peace to be shared between family members.

The Eucharist: The Mass is the summit of our lives, the most beautiful place on earth, a time when the heavens are open and communion between eternity and the Kingdom of God is total. Mass is an inexhaustible source for living each day in God's plan and discerning our ways from those of the Father. With the grace of the Eucharist, we become what we receive. Our mother's heart becomes little by little the image of God' heart. Our family gradually becomes a home in the Father's home.

When we go to Mass, let us choose our words. We enter the church and make the sign of the cross and genuflection: let us explain to our children that we are greeting Jesus who is there, near the little red light. Let us explain the meaning of our gestures, which are not a habit but a daily renewal of our Faith. Before or after Mass, let us go with our children to the tabernacle to exchange a word with Jesus. During the consecration, let us tenderly say to our child: "*Look carefully, Jesus is coming into the host and into your heart*". No need for long speeches, but a thousand invitations to look up to Heaven. The rest is the work of grace.

Confirmation: We are the temple of the Spirit. To care for our body, where the Spirit and his gifts dwell, is the duty of every Christian. This Spirit is alive in each member of our family, and each one carries different charisms. It is not a matter of putting labels on our children (whether negative or positive) but of helping each child to grow in the talents given to him or her by the grace of God.

Marriage: The love of the couple is the very image of Trinitarian love. "*God created man in the image of himself, in the image of God he created him, male and female he created them*" (Genesis 1:27). Let us take care of our couple. Let's make sure we have great respect for our spouse, and great tenderness and gentleness towards our spouse. Let us watch our language and the way in which we address the person whom the Lord has given us to walk towards Him on earth. Our spouse is given to us to sanctify us, and we ourselves are guardians of his or her soul to support him or her on the way. A solid couple is the most beautiful testimony of love and a great source of security, trust and comfort for our children.

Let us be careful with the vocabulary we use when we speak to our spouse, let us support each other, let us share what we are experiencing and feeling, let us encourage each other in our work and efforts, let us correct each other if necessary. The other is a sacred land that we must take great care of.

Ordination: A little aside, because this sacrament does not concern us directly, since we are mothers, but perhaps one of our children is called? Let us take care to awaken in them an availability to God's call, to make their hearts available to the call of their vocation, whether priestly, monastic or marital. Let us ask them about what they love, what matters to them, let us highlight their talents and the beautiful things they have accomplished, let us thank them for the outbursts of the heart that we witness. We prepare their land to respond to the vocation, religious or not, that the Lord has for them.

Let us pray to be enlightened and guide them according to the ways of the Lord, not according to our hopes. This is their only happiness on earth, to remain in the hands of the Father and to walk with His Son, in peace under the mantle of Mary who is the Holy Spirit.

The sacrament of the sick: This sacrament is not only for the end of our life but it is given by the Church to restore us after an illness or a deep suffering. This sacrament is there to heal us of our fears born or revealed in suffering (physical, psychological, moral suffering, trials of the soul). The enemy seeks to hide in the dark recesses of our heart, the sacrament of the sick comes to put light in us to raise us up.

No one can know what is really going on in someone's life. Some priests have the gift of sensing souls, but often they cannot guess in the square after Mass what is going on inside us or what pain we are going through.

A priest who knows us better, a spiritual director, a counsellor from a movement like the Teams of Our Lady or the Tandem Teams, a chaplain from a community, or a priest we met at a retreat, this person can offer us this sacrament. If not, let us have the humility to ask. It is a sacrament that we can receive several times in a lifetime, like the Eucharist and confession.

This sacrament has no magic effect, Faith is necessary, but the grace is real. Like all sacraments, it is a visible sign of the Father's love in our history.

The Lord has given priests a great gift in allowing them to administer the sacraments. Let us use them! Let us not refuse these gifts from Heaven! All of them, even the sacrament of the sick. The Lord will revive His spring in us if we come to him. He goes before us and calls us to join Him. Our tears will then have a different taste. Our tears will no longer be suffocating but liberating. Our suffering will be illuminated in the cross of Christ. We cannot guess at the fruits we bear in consenting to suffer for Christ, with Christ and in Christ. The fruits of the Father are far beyond us.

Let us not seek the benefits we have received, let us come for love of Him, to be with Him and let Him pour out His graces without counting the cost. Let us not doubt: He is at work, He is shaping us. In His time, He will offer us consolations according to our needs. Let us not seek them for their own sake, but give thanks for receiving them, for it does us good and encourages and sustains the action of grace within us.

In dry times, let us avoid making decisions with too much impact. Let us remain faithful and pray more. "*You should be awake, and praying not to be put to the test*" (Matthew 26:41). The Lord only allows moments of desolation to purify us, to prune that beautiful vine of our soul and to bring us closer to Him. Let us not try to understand or explain, our intelligence will never be equal to the intelligence and insight of God's heart. His disciples asked him, "*Rabbi, who sinned, this man or his parents, for him to have been born blind?' 'Neither he nor his parents sinned,' Jesus answered 'he was born blind so that the works of God might be displayed in him.*" (John 9:2-3). Let us trust. The Lord acts or allows certain events for His Glory.

Mission and vocation

The busier you are, the more important grace is. Put Christ first and He will even take care of the details of your life and schedule. Mass, silent prayer or prayer in general: never try to find out what you have got out of it, because then the enemy will come and whisper to you that you are wasting you time or that your prayer is not beautiful enough. These temptations are pure lies: the Lord does not need you to be "I am", but He thirsts for you, as you are. Christ does not come as a judge to check the length of your prayer time, your concentration or the beauty of your attitude. He comes to meet His sister in the depths of her heart.

God is in eternity. A notion difficult to grasp with our intelligence, however, I think that certain events in our life are really constitutive of who I am, of my unique and personal vocation in the heart of God. These small or big things in my history are my person, and that is how I will rise with my glorious body.

You must discern what is of the enemy and what is of the Spirit. What is of the Spirit remains and strengthens you in your mission. When you look back over your life, you see some key events that define you, characterise you or have transformed you. This is beautiful! Holiness is not the arduous or impossible climb up a mountain, earned by the sweat of your brow. Holiness is the daily bread given and shared out of love, with love and in love around you. This daily life, and these events of your daily life, of your vocation for today, which have happened in the past, now and tomorrow, are part of your eternity. You will rise on the last day with this, you will carry in your glorious body and your mother's heart the marks of those moments, those moments of eternity when you wanted to love in Truth.

Comforting a child, dressing a little one, feeding your family, visiting your parents, loving in the smallest things in your life as a mother, will give you the grace to love in the great things of God's eternity. How valuable your daily life, sometimes so simple and discreet, is in eternity! Mothers have a capacity to give themselves, to care, to love, to console, to listen, to encourage, to lift up that comes from the united hearts of Jesus and Mary.

What is your vocation? Pray, pray, pray to know it. The Lord calls you by the name your parents gave you on the day of your baptism. In his eternity, the Lord calls you by a word, that of your vocation in his divine plan. Listen to Saint Therese and the little way she chose: "*My vocation is love!*" Listen to St Francis of Assisi "*Lord, make me an instrument of your peace*" or the Holy Curé of Ars "*I love you, O my God, and my only desire is to love you to the last breath of my life*" or St Charles de Foucauld "*My Father, I abandon myself to You*". What about you? Christ speaks to you in your words, in your story, He reaches you, precedes you and calls you. Listen to Him. Simon becomes Peter in the heart of God. What about you? To what plan of love are you called for the glory of the Father?

Your vocation is there. Your mission begins here. Your vocation and your mission are a daily work for the greater Glory of God. With simplicity. In Truth. In the Spirit. Read again the Acts of the Apostles (1:8): "*You will receive power when the Holy Spirit comes on you*". In the same way, you are sent, first of all to your spouse, your family, and more widely to all the people who cross your path. Your vocation is blossoming. And Heaven has begun.

7-

Joy:

I have told you this so that my own joy may be in you

and your joy be complete (John 15:11)

I have the immense grace of having received joy at a very young age. It is a characteristic that was regularly noted. This joy was deepened as a teenager in gatherings like FRAT and WYD, with our dear Pope Saint John Paul II. This joy was reinforced by receiving the Sacrament of Confirmation, a high point in my life. But not everything was rosy. Echoing the previous chapter, joy has grown in me step by step and also through suffering. Each little cross was an opportunity to discover a new aspect of God's heart, to taste His peace, and to find comfort, to experience joy in everyday life.

True joy is the fruit of a life of faithfulness. The opposite of peace is not war. The opposite of peace is nothingness, for peace is fullness. The opposite of sin is not virtue. The opposite of sin is grace. We will not find joy by trying to do right and tick all the boxes. We will find true joy by leaving the door of our mother's heart open. We will find joy in asking Christ to fill us with his grace. We will find joy when we no longer seek pleasures, comfort or satisfaction, when we no longer seek reassurance or receive what we deem fair.

The Lord has put treasures in our hearts of which we only guess at a small part. Personally, I love to hear and receive the impulses of my children, such as spontaneously during a car journey "*I love how God created the world*" or a child lying on the floor drawing and saying softly "*I love you Mary*". What a joy to see how a child's heart is a privileged place to let God dwell in. It is up to us, mothers, to contemplate our little ones: this will awaken us to an education filled with gentleness, patience and tenderness. Our hearts will become soft, patient and tender, humble like a child's heart, to radiate the same joy as the crystalline laughter of our little ones.

The more we rely on our own strength, the more rigid and even fragile we become. Our mother's heart must learn to rely on others as well and to have the humility to ask for help. By remembering our weaknesses and accepting our limitations we learn to look kindly on the weaknesses and limitations of others. This is the first step in accepting that we can rest in God alone and look at the world through His merciful eyes.

Keep in mind that it is very brave to accept our limitations, to acknowledge our powerlessness. In the face of our smallness, we can become agitated, struggle with ourselves, feel so uncomfortable or begin to feel discouraged or even despair. Yet holiness does not lie in outbursts but in this lowliness, like the humble and meek lamb who gives us His peace. Holiness is not the stage that follows our temptations, difficulties or trials. Holiness is found in the midst of our temptations, difficulties and trials. It is rooted in our weakness. The idea is not to rejoice in being so limited as to absolve ourselves of not always trying to give our best. The idea is to recognise that our weaknesses allow God to work in us, allowing our barriers to fall away to make way for Him, to let Him work in us. Then God's heart shapes us in His image and comes to rest in our mother's heart.

Our mother's heart which unveils the heart of God very delicately, softly and in small steps, our mother's heart then becomes the temple of God's heart. There is no glitter here, it is true, but there is a lot of light. Jesus himself spent thirty years of life hidden away, in the ordinary day-to-day routine of family life. There is no greater proof that God the Father is totally united with every second of our life as mothers, given every moment in our home, in the hearts of each of its members.

We live in the present. I cannot relive yesterday and I cannot yet live tomorrow. I can only live, welcome and bless the present. Yet, being baptized, we have put on Christ and we are already in eternity. The Mass is the ultimate time when we access this eternity of love. The Mass is the ultimate time when we are united to eternity in the depths of our flesh, united in our bodies as women, wives and mothers with Jesus, through Jesus, in Jesus. The crosses in our lives are also doors to eternity. Our suffering has an end, but having suffered transforms us in depth and gives us eternal life. Then Christ's words resound: "*I have told you this so that my own joy may be in you and your joy be complete*" (John 15:11). This heavenly joy is a gift of eternity. It is not a question of earthly pleasures, satisfactions, comforts, worldly happiness or even justice, but of the joy of the angels, the saints, of Jesus himself who exults under the action of the Holy Spirit.

Do we realise that we are invited to this wedding? We are established to bear fruit and that our fruit remains. This fruit is the fruit of God. There is only humility in this, the fruit we bear is not our own and is not of our personal power. We are the branch that bears the fruit of God. Let us remain in Him, on the vine of Christ, and the fruits of the Father in us will be so tasty.

I spoke to you about sins in a previous chapter: the temptation of the enemy can creep into even a praiseworthy request in itself: to ask for an outpouring of the Spirit, a gift, a responsibility, a charism. Let us try to pray and express our requests to God with the glasses of humility on. Our works and the fruits we bear are only thanks to God, let us count nothing for ourselves, but in all things, let us give thanks and praise to the name of Jesus.

Let us pray, let us pray without ceasing. Let us pray for our children. Let us pray for our husband. Let us pray for ourselves. Let us ask for peace and joy in our family and in all the families of the world. If Jesus lived for thirty years hidden in the privacy of his family, our home too bears the seed of God's divinity. Family love is the image of Trinitarian love.

Jesus preached, healed, taught and travelled through his country and the surrounding countries for three years. In his footsteps, our family is invited to welcome, to shine, to set out on a journey for the glory of the Father.

Jesus suffered for three days, died, was crucified, went down to hell. Our family carries crosses, let us lay each one at the feet of Jesus on his cross so that they may be glorified and glorify the Father.

Jesus has risen, He has ascended into Heaven. He is in the eternity of love in the Father's house. Our family too is invited to be transformed, renewed, reborn of the Spirit. In eternity, we will all be reunited in the Father's house, fully ourselves and totally fulfilled. Our family bond will be magnified. There will be no more weeping. An eternity of peace and joy awaits us. This is our only goal. Let us keep our eyes and hearts firmly fixed on this one goal. This is our joy today. Let us stand ready and confident in the love of the

Father. In his hand we are unshakeable. We cannot imagine the blessings He is preparing for us and our family.

8-

Mary, her motherly heart

As a mother, I am at the same time the child that Christ lifts up in his arms to place him in the heart of the Father. And I am just as much the Christ who lifts his child to place him in the arms of God. And at the foot of this cross, who is there? A mother and her child. A child and his mother.

Mary is the best guide to understanding how to love God. She, the perfect heart who loved her Son so much, who knew the immense joy of seeing His glory and the wordless pain of witnessing His death, will be the perfect guide to teach you to love, to suffer and to give you His joy. Our Lady still weeps at times during certain apparitions, but this does not detract from her luminous beauty; she is the bride of the Holy Spirit.

Do not neglect your tears, the only danger would be to despair. Indeed, your suffering has great value. Mary had her heart pierced by a sword at the foot of the cross, but she was also there to see the birth of the universal Church. She was there to give comfort, encouragement and confidence that God takes care of everything and that all things work together for His Glory. Your mother's heart is invited to the same love: birth is a physical suffering and a supernatural joy, your life as a mother also invites your children to bring comfort, encouragement, and confidence. Ask Mary for her own heart to live in the heart of God. Whatever your joys and sorrows, she can comfort you. In her image, you become a first sign of God's tender love for your children.

At the foot of the cross, mother and son reunited at the feet of their Saviour, it is the Church that takes flesh. By this example, lean on the community of saints. The Church is your body. Your mother's heart, your family, your home are part of a whole. Ask your patron saints, the saints who are dear to you, your children already in the Glory of God to pray for you, to intercede to give you all the graces you need. Their prayers deposited in the eternity of the Kingdom of God are of a power you cannot imagine. United by the bond of love of those who have gone before you, your own prayer becomes part of the Kingdom of God. To such love the Father will refuse nothing. Thanks to this communion of the universal Church you will have full confidence: entrusting yourself above all to His will, you ask for His grace. Then you will receive treasures that will always be more beautiful than you could have imagined.

Sometimes, when things are going well or in the routine of everyday life, you may be tempted to look at your feet, or your navel. Change your perspective, look to Heaven. Suffering is terrible but the cross is your way of salvation, through it we are redeemed and saved. Mary, perfect immaculate, suffered so much; yet she remained firm and unfailing in her Faith, believing beyond all human understanding. This is your example. Your small and great sufferings invite you to look up to Heaven, to become aware that your life on earth is but a waiting room for eternal life. Like Mary, you become contemplative before the divine mystery. She who crushed the head of the serpent while turning her gaze towards the Father's house, your heavenly mother invites all mothers to join this eternity of joy.

Mary accepts for herself the Will of the Father, the Holy Trinity; she is covered with the mantle of the Holy Spirit, the Holy Trinity; Mary has carried in her womb Christ, the Holy Trinity.

You are a woman: this is the essence of your being, you carry within you a capacity to love and to give yourself without counting the cost;

you are a wife: as the Church is the wife of Christ, a wife who gives herself to her husband and welcomes life into her womb;

you are a mother: endowed with a heart called to tenderness, gentleness, patience, benevolence, and love overflowing for her children.

Your mother's heart is an instrument that reveals the heart of God, Trinitarian Love.

Magnificat

My soul proclaims the greatness of the Lord,
My spirit rejoices in God my Savior
For He has looked with favor on his lowly servant.
From this day all generations will call me blessed:
The Almighty has done great things for me,
And holy is his Name.
He has mercy on those who fear him
In every generation.
He has shown the strength of his arm,
He has scattered the proud in their conceit.
He has cast down the mighty from their thrones,
And has lifted up the lowly.
He has filled the hungry with good things,
And the rich he has sent away empty.
He has come to the help of his servant Israel
For he remembered his promise of mercy,
The promise he made to our fathers,
To Abraham and his children forever.
Glory be to the Father,
and to the Son,
and to the Holy Spirit.
As it was in the beginning,
is now,
and ever shall be,
world without end.
Amen.

Conclusion

The first commandment is: "*You must love the Lord your God with all your heart...*" (Matthew 22:37). Your heart is made to be the temple of the heart of Christ, you mothers are made to be a living tabernacle, shining in the world.

You are united to the heart of God when you carry the life He gives in your womb. You are united to the heart of Christ when you follow Him every day in your daily tasks and your maternal love, with humility in the simplest tasks, with dedication and kindness of heart in the most discreet things, with gentleness and patience to place the very love of God in the hearts of your children, to give them a foretaste of that much greater love to which we are all called. You are united in one Spirit when your family is a place of unity and peace, a place of acceptance of the other as he or she is, a place where your neighbour can regain his or her strength and continue on his or her way, rejuvenated by the warmth of your home.

St. John the Baptist said: "*He must grow greater, I must grow smaller*" (John 3:30). The path of a mother's life teaches us to become more and more self-effacing so as to ultimately see our children fly away, go on mission or join the Father's house. By diminishing, by finding true humility, the very heart of God grows in you. So no, it is not presumptuous to say that our heart as a mother is in the image of God's heart. The Father fashioned us in His image and gave us His Son. Without withholding anything of His Glory, He is humility itself, He gives us everything and invites us to come and rest in Him.

Let grace work in you, St John Paul II said: "*Open wide the doors to Christ, do not be afraid!*" Your heart will discover, step by step, bits and pieces of the love of the Most Holy Trinity so that you live fully in this infinite love, so that your heart no longer leaves the very heart of God.

I end with an image. I have always loved watching tree leaves move in the wind. Especially in spring, those leaves in such a rich range of green. If you look closely, you will see that each leaf moves differently. It's the same wind, but the movement of each one is unique.

When the tree is big, the wind can be different, it can blow harder at the top, at the bottom, on one side. Here again, each leaf moves differently, receives this wind in a unique way. They are always part of the tree, special, they are a testimony to the life of the tree. The soft green or darker green leaves, swaying in the breeze or whirling in the strong wind, hanging on the tree and in a general view, show its pure beauty. Each leaf contributes to the beauty of the tree.

Sometimes the leaves seem to stand still, their movement almost imperceptible. Time seems to stand still, waiting for the wind. Take time, look longer. A squirrel runs on a branch. You guess a bird singing. A pair of birds come courting each other, ready to give the life that comes with spring. These birds need the tree to shelter their nest. These chicks need the branches to grow up in a cosy and welcoming nest, before flying away to the sky and other horizons.

Look at the wind in the trees: each of their leaves is a reflection of a bridge between Heaven and Earth, just as your life here on earth is the heaven begun.

Prayer to Mary

Under the shelter of your mercy we take refuge,
Holy Mother of God.
Despise not our prayers when we are in trial, but from all dangers always deliver us, glorious and blessed Virgin.

Like this tree, seek refuge. Do not fear: your holy Mother has already crushed the head of the serpent. Place your children safely in her immaculate heart. Find in her her refuge. Your family will be ready for the wedding of the Lamb, watching and waiting for the return of the Master. Giving thanks for the fruits of your mother's heart, your family will enter the Glory of the Kingdom of Heaven, for an eternity of delight.

Author's note

I share here a little of my story and my thoughts born of my Faith. I write these lines with my heart, driven by the immense desire that the Father may find, in each of you, a place to rest and lay down His heart. He hopes only that you will open the door of your heart, that you will break down all barriers, to let the torrents of His infinite grace and love live in you. Decide to follow Him and then pray unceasingly for Him to dwell in you. In His time and according to His grace, I assure you that He will come and that all of Heaven will rejoice in your mother's heart united with His heart, the heart of God.

Table of contents

Acknowledgements 5

Preface 7

Introduction 11

1- From conception to birth 13

2- Our children, love in relationship 19

3- Ask for Faith.. 35

4- Prayer and spiritual warfare................................... 37

5- Suffering 47

6- The domestic church.. 61

7- Joy 71

8- Mary, her motherly heart 77

Conclusion 81

Author's note.. 85

About the author.. 89

About the author

Caroline Moulinet is a chemical engineer. She worked for several years in the cosmetics industry in France before moving to England. She is a mother of four children in a four years gap and she created Radiance Partners Ltd. to help women to fulfil their vocation as mothers. Lockdown is an opportunity for her to write: she is the author of the guide "*How to survive 14 days in isolation*" sold in France, the UK and the USA during the first lockdown. She continues to speak to mums with '*Pause, and change your perspective*', sharing her views on three key aspects of being a mum. This new book reveals some of the intimacy of her heart as a woman, wife and mother, and her relationship with God, Father, Son and Holy Spirit.

Printed in Great Britain
by Amazon